The House That ROSS BUILT

A step by step guide on how I built a successful house flipping business And how you can do the same

AZIZ ROSS

outskirts press

The House That Ross Built
A Step by Step Guide on How I Built a Successful House Flipping Business and How You Can Do the Same
All Rights Reserved.
Copyright © 2022 Aziz Ross
v2.0

The opinions expressed in this manuscript are solely the opinions of the author and do not represent the opinions or thoughts of the publisher. The author has represented and warranted full ownership and/or legal right to publish all the materials in this book.

This book may not be reproduced, transmitted, or stored in whole or in part by any means, including graphic, electronic, or mechanical without the express written consent of the publisher except in the case of brief quotations embodied in critical articles and reviews.

Outskirts Press, Inc.
http://www.outskirtspress.com

ISBN: 978-1-9772-5584-6

Cover Photo © 2022 Aziz Ross. All rights reserved - used with permission.

Outskirts Press and the "OP" logo are trademarks belonging to Outskirts Press, Inc.

PRINTED IN THE UNITED STATES OF AMERICA

DISCLAIMER

This book is meant to be a step-by-step guide to do your first flip and begin to build a real estate investment empire. This will aid you in accomplishing that. Although the easy process laid out will aid you in doing that, by no means is this some magical recipe for success in real estate or anything else for that matter. Every chapter and step requires action and a willingness to learn even further; without that it's just another how-to book that sits on your shelf with no result. If you don't intend to take action, either immediately or in the foreseeable future, then don't waste your time reading it. If it is, then continue to read and realize your dream. Good luck, one way or the other (even though it will take more than luck).

REAL ESTATE TERMS YOU NEED TO KNOW

1. ARV- after repair value
2. Realtor- someone who sells or helps you buy a house
3. Contractor- someone or company that provides labor or service, (in this case remodeling or construction service)
4. REIA- real estate investors association
5. Hard Money Lender- a company that lends money for investment properties
6. Private Capital- private investments en-compassing the follow- asset class (in this case real estate)
7. Investor- someone who provides or invests money or resources for or to an enterprise or project.
8. Flipping/Rehabbing- in simple terms, to fix a distressed property
9. Wholesaler- someone who sells, in this case a property, to an investor at a lower than retail price
10. ROI- return on investment
11. Capital- money invested or available for investment
12. Appraisal- assessment of the value of the property
13. Inspection- the action of examining a property for its condition
14. Survey- the action of confirming a property's boundary lines and legal description
15. Property title- is a document that shows legal ownership to a property
16. Title insurance- insures against financial loss from defects in title to real property and from the invalidity of mortgage loans
17. Mortgage- is a loan used by purchasers of real property
18. Homeowners Association (HOA)- is a private association-like entity formed for the purpose of managing homes in a residential subdivision
19. HUD Statement- is a standardized mortgage lending form on which creditors or their closing agents itemize all charges imposed on buyers and sellers in a mortgage transaction
20. Closing- the document signing and transfer of ownership

Table of Contents

1. Mindset 1
2. You Make Money in Real Estate when You Buy, Not When You Sell 4
3. Establishing Your Business & LLC 6
4. Raising Capital 8
5. How to Finance Your Properties 10
6. Finding Properties 12
7. Evaluating a Property 14
8. Rehabbin/Repairing Your Flip 17
9. Conclusion 23

CHAPTER 1

MINDSET

THE MOST IMPORTANT thing in all of this is mindset. How and what you think will determine your success in this and in any objective in life. For instance, a person who has been an employee their whole life will think about earning and getting paid for every hour of work they do. In real estate and in any business: you work, do more work, then you do some more work, and, finally, you get paid. This is a tough reality for most people to under-stand; that's why most start and quit after trying for a short period. That's the first mistake: people **TRY**. The way I see it, either you make a commitment to make it work or you don't. So let's take **TRY** out of our vocabulary right now. That's the first tip among several I'm going to give you in developing a winning mindset. Along with taking **TRY** out of your vocabulary, you will need to start being more confident of what you say. From now on only speak of what you want and who you want to be or do, as if you are already doing it or have it. I will explain further in the next tip. Tip two: positive affirmations. I want you to write out a list of things you are wanting to accomplish. As I mention in step one, you need to write them as if you're almost there or are doing it presently. Speak what you want, not what you have. Your affirmations will need to start with: "I have," "I am" and sometimes "I will." For example "I am flipping five houses a month." "I have $100k in cash flow a year into my real estate business." "I will take action now to achieve my goals," so on and so forth. I just gave you examples about real estate, but you should also do this in other areas of your life. Don't be afraid to aim high, but at the same time don't be unrealistic. Base everything on where you are starting from. You need both mind and motivation to be able to believe that whatever you state is doable. As you develop yourself, your skills and your mindset, then you can expand your goals. That will be different for every individual based on their confidence and place in life. The belief part will take a while, but eventually you will believe it and realize you can achieve it. After you've written out your affirmations, you need to repeat them to yourself out loud or in your head a minimum of three times a day, every day. Once in the morning when you wake up, once midday, and once before you go to sleep at night. I said a minimum, but I want you to realize that the more you repeat them the faster you will believe that you can accomplish them. The faster you believe them, the faster you will start taking action to accomplish them. The reason why this is effective is because your subconscious mind doesn't know the difference between what's reality and what's not. It acts on what you tell it and believe. This is a key concept to understand in the process of changing your mindset. There are many books and other resources which allow you to do your own research about this concept. I advise you to take a little time to do some research on the topic. Tip three is goal-setting. This step can actually be done before or after tip two. I will cover this briefly, because goal-setting is a skill that will need to be studied and developed over time. I believe people who don't really learn the skill totally fail in achieving their goals and don't understand why. Goal-setting goes hand in hand with affirmations. The difference is that affirmations are a shorter version of your goal which is said daily to develop the thoughts in your mind, to activate the brain, and to take action regarding what you aim to accomplish. A goal is a more defined set of plans including how and what you want to accomplish. It's reviewed occasionally over a period of time—for example on a monthly or quarterly basis. The first thing you must keep in mind about goal-setting is that you need to be as specific as possible. It's not enough to say: "I want to start a real estate business." It would need to sound more like this, "I am starting a real estate business January 1, 2022. The main focus of my business is flip-ping houses in the Houston, Texas area. After I flip ten houses there, I will branch out to other places around the country."

I think you get the point.

The other important part about goal-setting is that sometimes you may not hit the goal when you expected. That doesn't mean you should beat yourself up about it or get discouraged. It means you might have missed something or the timing wasn't right. Just reset the goal, learn why you didn't hit it and work on that, so you will hit the new goal. This may happen several times. Doesn't matter. Just keep hitting reset and if you don't quite reach it, eventually you will. Tip five: Read. This needs to become a habit, something you do every day. You need to set a specific time you read this on a daily basis. I suggest you read in the morning when you get up and then at night before you go to sleep. I suggest this for many reasons, but most importantly I believe that reading in the morning helps you get a positive start to your day. This will help you keep a positive attitude when you face negative situations and people throughout the day. The reason to read at night before you go to sleep is so you can end your day on a positive note. Also reading before you go to sleep allows your sub-conscious mind to remember and process the information as you sleep. The last and final tip, which I believe is the most important, is narrowing down your reason **WHY**. You will need to establish a very strong reason **WHY** you want to make money investing in real estate. Quick example would be, "I want to make money in real estate to buy a new house or take care of my parents, or travel the world, etc." Your reason **WHY** is what is going to keep you going until you reach your goal. Without it you will probably quit. All in all, when you do the things laid out in the tips above, you will develop the mindset to win, and as stated at the beginning of this chapter the mindset is where it all begins.

CHAPTER 2

YOU MAKE MONEY IN REAL ESTATE WHEN YOU BUY, NOT WHEN YOU SELL

ONE HUGE MISCONCEPTION that people believe is that you make money when you sell a property or rent it out. I'm here to change that belief. Here's why: because it's wrong. Let me explain why I say that. It actually goes against what would seem logical.

When you sell or rent out a property, you do get paid. How much profit you make or don't make depends strictly on how much you paid for the property. Also depends on how much money you have to invest in the property to fix it up. For example let's say I buy a property for $100,000 and it's going to cost me $30,000 to rehab, so I'll be all in at $130,000. The ARV (after repair value) is $170,000 so in this example, excluding closing costs, carrying cost, etc., to keep things simple, I make $40,000 Not bad, right? But let's give you the flip side of that. Let's say I buy the same property for $145,000, and set a budget for re-hab at $30,000. The ARV is the same $170,000, so in this example I would lose $5,000.

Although this is an extreme example. I hope you can see now why I say you make money when you buy and not when you sell.

YOU MAKE MONEY IN REAL ESTATE WHEN YOU BUY, NOT WHEN YOU SELL

You get paid when you sell based on what you bought it for, which can result in a profit or a loss. Although this is a book about fix and flip/flipping, I will give you a brief explanation regarding how this holds true for buy and hold/rental property. When you pay too much for a rental property and your mortgage/ expenses exceed what you get in rent, then you end up losing money on a monthly basis for the property. When you buy it right and your mortgage/expenses are less than you receive in rent, then you make a profit monthly. You would be surprised by how many people starting out or even some who have actually done a few deals but don't get this. But it doesn't take them long to understand it, because the industry helps them realize this real fast and they go broke. Again, hope this all makes sense, because it's one of the most important aspects of investing in real estate.

CHAPTER 3

ESTABLISHING YOUR BUSINESS & LLC

NOW THAT WE'VE got the pre-business and mindset stuff done, we can dig into getting your business started. First, you need to think of a name for your business. The name should be general and should not in any way have the word "investment" attached to it. I will explain why in a few. What I mean by general, for example is AB Enterprises, Llc or Light House Industries, Llc. I wouldn't suggest you use your name unless it's abbreviated or simply your initials. You don't want the public to know you are the owner.

Unfortunately in our society there are people that prey on others and look for ways to take what you've built, so stay away from using your name as your business name. Now to address why I say don't use the word "investment" in your name. Eventually you will want to borrow money for your business and 95% of institutions will not loan to real estate investment companies in particular. It's the hardest loan to get. I'm speaking from firsthand experience, as you'll see when you read on. I'm not speaking theory or what I think. Everything written in the pages of this book I've done or am doing now. The first company I started included "investments" as part of the name and because of that I couldn't get a general business loan although I had good credit and good revenue history. I later learned why, when I took a business credit-building class: my business name was the problem. The most unfortunate thing about it was that I built a pretty solid business for years before I figured this out, and at that point I was kind of stuck with the name. I created a DBA (doing business as), but it's not the same as operating an LLC. Hope my experience helps drive home the point. Side note: you can do okay using "Capital" but I would avoid using that also. In any case, take some time and choose your name wisely.

The last part in building your business and probably the most important part is building your team. Start immediately if you are serious about getting into this business. You are going to need people on your team that have experience in different areas, which will lessen the gap of your inexperience. Who do you want as a part of your team? That can vary based on your experience and what things you've done in real estate up to this point. In general you will need a real estate agent, accountant, contractors, hard money lender/mortgage lenders, title company, marketing team or company and if at all possible a mentor that has been doing real estate for at least a few years. Some of your team members you will need right away and others you'll need later on in the process. Having this established beforehand will greatly improve your chances for success.

CHAPTER 4

RAISING CAPITAL

R AISING CAPITAL IS the next step in the process of building your real estate business. This will be a skill that you will continue to grow over the years. I will guide you in how to get started, but because this is a very in-depth process, I have an entire book coming out soon that will cover it in detail.

First thing you need to know is that you shouldn't feel like you're asking for help. You are providing people with an opportunity to make passive income and you should approach it as such. Look at it as a win/win situation for you and for them.

Again this is a mindset. From this day forth you are a real estate investor, and you need to start telling people you are. When you start speaking it, people will start asking about it. When they do, let them know you are working on flipping houses. Ask if they would be interested in making some extra money investing with you on some flips. Tell them you will handle all the work. All they have to do is put up some money. They will ask you how much they need to invest, and I want you to respond with $2500 minimum. The next question they will ask is what their return will be (ROI). The response to that is about 10%-30%, depending on the deal. Start doing this the minute you finish this chapter. Who should you ask? I want you to start by asking friends, family, coworkers, etc., basically people you already know. As you get people that show an interest, start creating a list of those names to call on when you're ready. Once you get about ten names give or take, I want you to start calling them and let them know you are getting ready to close on a deal. Ask them if they would be interested in investing $5k on the deal. I advise you to start there, so you have some wiggle room to ask for less if $5k is too much. If so then ask them if they could do $2500. For the ROI tell them 15%, start here so you can tell them 20% or more if they act like 15% isn't enough. Let them know the turnaround will be about four months (time period may vary depending on the property, but this is the average time it takes to rehab and sell a property). I know this may seem like a lot based on a four-month turnaround but you must realize you are just getting started and you want to build relationships. Once you execute on your first deal and you pay off your investors, you will have investors lined up for all your deals. Once you get some people who say they want to invest, let them know as soon as the deal is locked in that you will send them a contract. Now you will need to create a contract if you don't already have one. I would suggest you have a lawyer or someone who is familiar with how a contract should be drafted to write it up. It will probably only cost you about $500-$700, which is cheap based on how much money it will help you make, as well as the protection it will give you. Besides that it will look professional, which makes you look professional. I paid $700 to have mine done and I've been using the same one for years.

    Next you must find a deal. I will cover the how-to in the next couple of chapters. Start sending out the contracts so you can have the money to put down to purchase the property. On average you will need about $25-$30K to put down.

CHAPTER 5

HOW TO FINANCE YOUR PROPERTIES

FINDING A LENDER should be easy if you have a good deal. Before I explain, realize that getting loans for your deals should be temporary. Eventually, once you get enough capital from investors as well as your own capital you should be paying for your deals with cash. There are multiple ways to find lenders. First, we will talk about traditional lenders. Obviously we're talking about the type of lender with whom you have your personal home mortgage. This type of lender will give you the best rate, but may be more difficult to deal with. They will require a good credit score, a good debt-to-income ratio, and at least 10% down. They usually won't lend you the money to do the repairs, so you will need to have your own money for that. Unless you have these things in place already, this probably will not be the type of lender for you. Most likely you will need to use what we call in the industry "hard money" or fix and flip loans. It's very expensive, but most don't require much to get a loan. The main criteria they are concerned with is the property. What I mean by that is they want to know if the property has equity or value above and beyond your own purchasing price. This is the after-repair value or ARV. Remember earlier when I spoke about making money when you purchase, not when you sell. Well, here is another example where that is true. Hard money lenders loan you on the ARV and it's usually about 70%. That means if you purchase a property for $50k and the ARV is $125k this is also the price you will probably sell the property for. The hard money lender will loan you $87,500 which will cover the purchase of the property as well the rehab cost. Note the repair money will be distributed in what is called a draw. Your hard money lender will explain how this works. Essentially in this example you would likely only have to pay out of pocket a couple of thousand or less for closing costs. This type of deal is what investors refer to as no-money-down deals. Again, you make money when you buy the property. I hope you are getting the point. If not you're going to hear it several more times, lol. At one point or another you are probably going to deal with a hard money lender if you plan on doing multiple properties at once. That is, unless you are capital heavy or can get a big investor. This is possible if you follow the steps in the previous chapter.

CHAPTER **6**

FINDING PROPERTIES

NOW THAT WE'VE discussed how to fund your properties, let's get into how to find a property. First thing I always suggest to new investors is to start looking at as many properties as possible. You can do this on line through multiple sources. You can reach out to a realtor and ask him or her to send you properties. That realtor can also take you out so you can see some properties physically. You can talk to some wholesalers and ask them to send you properties. The idea here is to look at all kinds of properties, some that have already been rehabbed, some that need to be rehabbed, and everything in between. The other important thing to remember about this is that you want to be specific about the properties you look at, such as the area you want to invest in, the price range you want to be in, and so on. Quick tip about the price range: you want to be in the low- to mid-range prices based on your market and area. The reason for this is because this is where a large part of the buyers fall in, which gives you a better chance of success to sell your properties fast. Also it means less risk for you, because the amount of capital to invest in most of these types of properties is low. Again, (I bet you know what I'm going to say) you make money when you buy, not when you sell. The reason you want to look at a lot of properties before you buy one is so you know what to look for and how it should look once you rehab it, based on your area and price range. Most

FINDING PROPERTIES

times when you are starting out you probably want to use a wholesaler to find your first property. It's a little more expen-sive but the benefits outweigh the expense. Wholesalers in most cases are experienced in finding distressed properties, and also give you a ball park range of what your rehab will cost as well as what your ARV will be. There are also multiple other ways to find properties on your own, which is ok too. It may take you a little longer but if you've looked at enough of them before, you should know what to look for. The other ways to look for properties are skip-tracing, which means getting a foreclosure list from your county or city or from a company that compiles them and sells the list. You can target probates; you can also buy a list of these from companies as well. You can focus on REO or banked-owned properties which a realtor can help you find, or again you can purchase a list of them from some of the same companies that sell the other list. The beautiful thing about using the in-ternet is that you can find all of these options by just doing a search on your phone or computer. You can also join a local REIA group and find all these resources. If you go the route of finding your own properties, there is another set of skills you will need to have. You will need to be able to communicate and negotiate with the homeowners after you get whatever list you want to work from. That's the nice thing about working with a wholesaler, because he or she has already done this by the time they send you the property. That's a decision you will have to determine from the start: are you ready to find your own deal or pay a little more and work with a wholesaler? I just made a suggestion based on what I did, but everyone is different and has to decide what works best for them. There are other ways to find deals that are a little more complex. I just gave you the most popular and easiest ones, especially for those just starting out.

CHAPTER 7

EVALUATING A PROPERTY

AFTER YOU HAVE looked at many properties and have determined which method you're going to use to find your deals, you need to evaluate the property to see what number makes sense to pay for the property. To do that you need to first go through the properties you have from your list and narrow them down to the ones on which you want to move forward. This is important, because you can waste a lot of time looking at properties that have little or no profit potential. The easiest way to do this is to put the properties in categories based on price and ARV. The rule of thumb in doing fix & flip deals is your purchase price and rehab cost should fall in at 70% of the ARV. This can vary slightly based on the deal and the current market situation. You can get the ARV number from your realtor by asking them to do a comparable analysis report (comps). You can do a quick check yourself by doing an internet search by the property zip code and see what's for sale in the nearby area. Here are a couple of examples to illustrate this method. From your list you see a property that's for sale at $100k and the ARV is $180k. Multiply the ARV by 70% and that equals $126k (The max you can pay including repairs +/-). Without yet knowing the amount for repairs needed in this example you would keep this property on the potential list. In another example you see a property for sale for $100k and the ARV is $135K. Multiply that by 70% and you get $94,500 (the max you can pay including repairs +/-). This is too far from the 70% margin, and you still haven't figured in the repair cost.

This property would go in your trash list. There will be some properties that are borderline which fall in like 70-75%. I would keep those on your potential list until you see what your repair costs will be. Using this method is how you can assess properties quickly and will save you a lot of time chasing properties that aren't any good. Okay, so now you have a list of several properties that have potential. The next step is too physically go out to the property so you can see what repairs need to be done. As you become accomplished at evaluating the repairs that are needed you can have someone like your realtor go out to the property either in person or remotely as they walk the property and show you both advantages and repair problems. That's down the road but it's cool when you get to that point because now you are systemizing your business. Next, for the first few properties you acquire you need to go out physically, preferably with a contractor, unless you have remodeling or construction experience. Your contractor will be able to point out approximate repair costs and help you create a solid budget. After you go out with him or her several times, you should get better at seeing what needs to done and at creating a budget. On your first walk-through you should take a repairs/budget list to check off and take notes with you, so you can use the list to help you get an idea of what to look for. You can get a repair/budget list from your contractor or from your hard money lender if you are working with one. Keep in mind when you are doing your walk-through what your budget is.

This should be determined by the 70% method we discussed earlier. You don't want to go into a property without knowing this, or you will end up over-rehabbing or paying too much. Over-rehabbing is a common mistake for new flippers. Remember you have a budget and you want to stick with it. You are not living in the property, so it's not based on what you like or want; it's based on the other properties in the neighborhood and industry trends. When I see people ignore this rule they either miss out on buying a good property or buy the property and go over their budget. Now there are some instances in which the needed repairs exceed your initial budget. In this case, since you know your numbers going in, you would just offer less. If they take it, great; if not great. At least you know you're not getting into a bad deal. You already know what I'm going to say: "You make money when you buy, not when you sell."

CHAPTER **8**

REHABBING/REPAIRING YOUR FLIP

REHABBING IN REAL estate is a term for repairing a property. Once you get to this point you're on your way to completing your first deal, as I mentioned in the previous chapter. The key thing is to stick to the budget that you created when you did your walk-through as closely as possible. A lot of times there will be unexpected issues that come up. This is normal so don't panic. What I do and suggest to others is to keep an extra $5k aside for when, not if, this happens. Something will come up about 90% of the time, so it's better to be prepared mentally and financially. Starting out you need to schedule and line things up so you can start the day you close on the property, or at least the next day.

The rest of this chapter is going to explain how to do this as well as how to manage the whole pro-cess step by step. It's very important to manage your rehab well. Actually it's the most important part of the rehab process, especially if you're dealing with hard money lenders, because this is how you will get the money for the repairs which are crucial to keep the rehab from lasting forever. Your hard money lender will explain how the draw process works. A big part of this is staying on top of your contractors. I'm going to say this again: stay on top of your contractors, especially on your first home so they know what you will expect on-going. In most cases this is the first time you have worked with this person, so you won't know how reliable they are or what quality of work they do. When we talked about building your team this is going to be one of the most important team members you have in my opinion. I suggest you have several on your team in case one doesn't work out. In a lot of cases this will be true and you will need to replace one with another. I believe finding good reliable and reasonably priced contractors is the hardest part of the whole flipping process. You will probably go through a few before you find the right one. That's coming from my experience, as well as experiences from others I've mentored into the business. This is why I say you need to stay on top of them. When they don't get work done in a quality or timely manner (unless there is a good reason), you need to replace them. When they say they're going to be there and they don't show up, get rid of them (again, unless it's a good reason and that good reason is only valid once). The second time, let them go. If the quality of work is sub-par and you let them know they need to do it over and they start telling you it's going to cost more, get rid of them. If they tell you one price and then weeks later they tell you a higher price get rid of them, (unless, of course, you change the scope of work or add something else). I think you see the point here.

You can't give them a lot of chances so be stern. If the rehab bogs down or is poorly done it can ruin your whole project. I've been there, so learn from what I'm telling you so you don't make the same mistake.

Now that this is understood let's continue the step-by-step process of flipping a house after it's acquired. I'll start with what you should do a few days before closing.

1. Schedule a dumpster to be delivered on closing date.
2. Schedule demolition guys to meet you at the property the day of or the next morning after you close.
3. Schedule electric to be turned on.
4. Schedule water to be turned on unless there are plumbing

REHABBING/REPAIRING YOUR FLIP

issues that will cause water damage.
(Have someone there when it's turned on just in case there's a leaky or busted pipe you didn't notice originally).

Funny story about the second property I did. I had the water turned on and wasn't there. When I showed up at the property that evening about a half inch of water had spread throughout the main bathroom and main bedroom. I spent all night vacuuming up the water with a wet dry vac. This is the first time I shared this story so don't tell anyone else. Don't worry. You'll have funny stories just like this to tell after you've done a few. But that's ok, the best teachers sometimes are our own mistakes or failures. I wouldn't have been able to give you a heads up on this if I never went through it, so it was a profitable experience overall. Alright, enough about my mistakes. Now we will cover the process once you close on the house. You should have already laid out what repairs are needed and you're ready to start

1. Demolition and Clean up - (everything should be cleared out before you move to the next step)

2. Plumbing- is next because sometimes you will have to open or remove drywall

3. Electrical- can be done at the same time as plumbing if you like. Sometimes your electrician will also have to remove drywall 4. Framing, drywall, interior doors and trim- sometimes you will have to do some framing in conjunction with the plumbing and electric

1. Tape Float and Sand - basically this is done to get drywall ready for paint.

2. Wall texture- This step varies based on your geographical region. Mostly popular in your southern regions.

3. **Paint**

4. **Bathrooms**- tub surround tile, bathroom floor tile, toilet installation, shower door (if you're replacing tub it should be done with plumbing) *Quick tip: depending on the price point which should be on the low to mid-low and the tub is not in really bad shape, like it doesn't have dents and big scratches, you should just have it resurfaced. Saves a lot of money and time.

5. **Kitchen Cabinets and Counter Tops**

6. **Lighting**- this includes ceiling fans and all additional lighting fixtures that were not done with the electrical work (you do this toward the end, so you don't get paint on or damage the finish lighting).

7. **Roof**- this is gauged on a need-by-need basis, because often you will not have to replace the roof, if it's in decent shape. You can just have it power washed. Obviously if it leaks you would need to replace it and if it does, this should be done at the same time as step one or before so that water doesn't get into the house.

8. **Siding, wood trim and brick repair or replacement if needed.**

9. **Exterior Paint**

10. **Windows**- a word of advice that I learned early on. Don't replace windows unless absolutely necessary. If they open, close, lock, and are not cracked, then don't replace them. Have them washed really well and if a buyer asks you to replace them just give them a credit (about half), of

REHABBING/REPAIRING YOUR FLIP

the cost of replacing them. You save a couple of thousand dollars and they can get their own when they are ready. I hardly ever replace windows unless it's a complete gut job or a higher-end house. This should not be an issue for you, because you shouldn't be doing higher-end on your first few anyway.

11. Landscaping- grass, if needed, flower beds, mulch, shrubs etc. you shouldn't spend more than $300 on landscaping.

12. Floors and carpet- this is always one of the last steps, because your contractors will mess them up when they're working. I do carpet in the bedrooms, laminate in the living rooms, and hallways, and tile in the kitchen and bathrooms (which could also be done when you're doing the bathrooms and kitchen if you prefer). I say this because tile is easy to clean and harder to damage.

13. Punch List- this is a term used in construction, that means all left-over finish work that wasn't done (like door knobs, door stops, battery operated smoke detectors, touch up paint, small dings and scratches, crooked tile, final clean up, etc.) This step should be done before you make the final payment to your contractor. At this point you and your contractor will do a final walk-through of the property with a roll of blue tape marking everything you see that still needs to be done. That way the contractor doesn't miss anything. Once the contractor corrects and completes all these items, then you can give him his final payment.

14. Power Washing- as I mentioned before, if you don't replace the roof you should power wash it. You will also need to power wash the driveway and sidewalks around the house as well as any places that might have gotten dirt on them like the garage door or bottom of the house.

15. Take pictures- I usually use a professional photographer (that costs about $100-$150). Nowadays with the quality of cameras and smart phone cameras, you can do it yourself if you prefer to save a few bucks.

16. Realtor walk-through- this is the last and final step before you list the property. This is done so you and your realtor can figure out a listing price, also so you can show and explain to the realtor everything that was done so he or she can do the write up and be familiar with the work when showing clients.

That's it! Now the realtor can list the property. Closing note on this chapter: The things on the repair list are based on how I do my flips. This can vary depending on your preference and your region. For example, you might want to start on the outside and then work your way inside. One thing that I didn't mention on the list is foundation repair. This will also vary depending on your region. When I do properties in Houston and the surrounding areas, foundation issues are almost always a part of my repairs and are no big deal to me or the end buyer, because it's common in that area due to all the rain. On the flip side of that, I also do properties in the Washington, DC metro area commonly called the DMV (DC, Maryland, Virginia) for those that are familiar with that area. Foundation issues are uncommon and will make it hard for you to sell even if you repaired it and gave a warranty. For that reason I would not do a house in that area that had a foundation problem. Again, if a region doesn't have periodic flooding issues then a foundation issue may become a real headache.

CHAPTER 9

CONCLUSION

NOW THAT EVERYTHING is basically laid out for you to start your flipping/real estate business, you have no excuses. You should be starting your business now that you have finished this book if not before. The hardest part is the first step and the most difficult flip will be your first one. Once you get through that you will be more at ease.

Let me paint a picture to help build your dream. As I write this book I'm sitting out front of a local coffee shop, while my guys are working on the different houses I'm doing now. I started out the day going for a ride on my bike to get some exercise. After that I had a few conference calls and then went to check on the progress of one of my projects. That was the most work I did all day outside of doing some writing to finish this book. Not all days are like this. Some days I do even less lol, but really that's true and other days are long and hard. More are easy than hard, and it will be the same for you. This is not an overnight process but I'm sure if you follow the steps you've learned in this book you can do it. It doesn't take some unique skill or ability. All it takes is the proper mindset, a willingness to learn and sometimes fail or make mistakes. Outside of this book you can follow my podcast THE BLACK INVESTORS for additional tips on Spotify or wherever you listen to your podcast. Also I have a private Facebook group (www.facebook.com/groups/ building-withross) where you can ask questions and get support from me and others that are doing their first projects or that have done several.

www.ingramcontent.com/pod-product-compliance
Lightning Source LLC
Chambersburg PA
CBHW031518210526
45464CB00007B/2968